ADHD

ANN O. SQUIRE

Children's Press®
An Imprint of Scholastic Inc.

Content Consultant

Phyllis Meadows, PhD, MSN, RN
Associate Dean for Practice
Clinical Professor, Health Management and Policy
University of Michigan
Ann Arbor, Michigan

Library of Congress Cataloging-in-Publication Data
Names: Squire, Ann, author.
Title: ADHD / by Ann O. Squire.
Other titles: True book.
Description: New York, NY : Children's Press, an imprint of Scholastic Inc., 2016. | Series: A true
    book | Includes bibliographical references and index.
Identifiers: LCCN 2015048545| ISBN 9780531228425 (library binding) | ISBN 9780531233269 (pbk.)
Subjects: LCSH: Attention-deficit hyperactivity disorder—Juvenile literature.
Classification: LCC RJ506.H9 S665 2016 | DDC 618.92/8589—dc23
LC record available at http://lccn.loc.gov/2015048545

© 2017 Scholastic Inc.
All rights reserved. Published in 2017 by Children's Press, an imprint of Scholastic Inc.
Printed in China 62
SCHOLASTIC, CHILDREN'S PRESS, A TRUE BOOK™, and associated logos are trademarks and/or
registered trademarks of Scholastic Inc.
1 2 3 4 5 6 7 8 9 10 R 26 25 24 23 22 21 20 19 18 17

Front cover: A frustrated boy at school
Back cover: A child shaking his head in confusion

Find the Truth!

Everything you are about to read is true *except* for one of the sentences on this page.

Which one is **TRUE**?

T or F   There is only one type of ADHD.

T or F   Experts do not fully understand what causes ADHD.

Find the answers in this book.

Contents

THE **BIG** TRUTH!

Famous Folks With ADHD

Albert Einstein

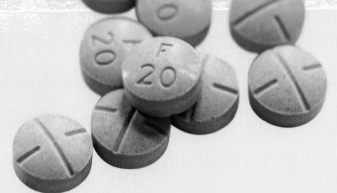

Adderall is a stimulant drug commonly used to treat ADHD.

Children playing

Some students have a very hard time focusing on what their teacher is saying.

CHAPTER 1

What Can It Be?

Brian's third-grade class was working on math. The teacher had written a problem on the board. Everyone was writing, trying to figure out a solution. Everyone but Brian, that is. He had started working on the problem but couldn't really focus on it. He hadn't been listening when the teacher explained what they should do. Now he was gazing out the window, watching cars and trucks go by on the street outside the school.

Problems in school can be a clue that a child may have ADHD.

Struggling in School

"Brian! Brian, do you hear me?" The teacher's voice jolted Brian out of his daydream. She didn't sound happy. She scolded him for not paying attention again. Brian could hear kids whispering. He knew they thought he was lazy, maybe even stupid. Brian felt bad. He wanted to do well in school, but he just didn't know how. Listening and paying attention seemed easy for everyone else. But for Brian, they were impossible.

It can be embarrassing to get caught daydreaming in school.

Kids who goof around in class can distract other students from learning.

The class next door was facing a different problem. Carl was being disruptive again. Everyone thought of him as the "class clown." Carl squirmed, bounced up and down, and yelled out answers instead of raising his hand. Whenever another student tried to speak, Carl would interrupt excitedly.

"Carl! Please calm down or I'll have to send you to the principal!" the teacher warned. Carl didn't want that. But as hard as he tried, he just couldn't stop fidgeting.

A disruptive student's parents might be called in to talk to a teacher, principal, or counselor.

CHAPTER 2

Making a Diagnosis

A few weeks later, Brian's and Carl's parents visited the school counselor to discuss their child's behavior. The boys behaved very differently, but both had trouble getting along with other kids. Both had difficulties with schoolwork. They both also took up so much of a teacher's time that the rest of the class suffered. The counselor suspected that the boys might have a **disorder** called attention deficit/**hyperactivity** disorder (ADHD).

Parents, teachers, and counselors work together to **diagnose** and manage a child's ADHD.

Different Symptoms

Carl's parents were not happy to hear this suggestion, but they had to admit it was a possibility. Carl was very active and had trouble sitting still even at home. He wasn't good at following instructions, and he frequently had tantrums, or "meltdowns." Brian's parents, on the other hand, were surprised. Brian was hardly hyperactive. He was forgetful, distracted, and had a tendency to daydream. He often seemed to be lost in his own world.

Kids with ADHD may become upset very suddenly.

Dealing with death or loss can bring on symptoms similar to those seen in ADHD.

Diagnosing ADHD

There is no single test to determine whether a person has ADHD. Hyperactive or **inattentive** behaviors can have a range of causes. One possibility is a change in family structure, such as a death or divorce. Physical causes include an ear infection that affects hearing. Anxiety, depression, **learning disabilities**, and other medical problems affecting the brain may mimic ADHD. The first step in diagnosing ADHD, therefore, is to rule out other causes.

Seeing a doctor is often the first step toward diagnosing ADHD.

Both families made appointments with their doctors. The doctors did physical exams and asked about any previous injuries, especially head injuries. Both boys seemed to be in good health, and no physical problems were detected. The doctors recommended the families see a specialist, or expert, who is trained to diagnose ADHD. The families could visit psychiatrists, psychologists, social workers, or licensed counselors.

The families made appointments with different specialists. Both experts explained that there are several things to look for when ADHD is suspected. The first is whether the problem behaviors are beyond what is normal for the person's age. Many kids are very active and excitable, and many find it hard to pay attention. However, not all kids have ADHD. A child with ADHD shows those traits much more than others who are the same age.

It is normal for kids to be playful and have lots of energy.

An ADHD specialist also looks at how recently the behaviors began. Have they been going on for a long time, or are they a response to a recent change in the child's life? For an ADHD diagnosis, a child must have shown symptoms for at least six months. They must also occur in different settings, such as at home, at school, and in social situations.

A child who is overly active on the playground but behaves normally everywhere else would not be diagnosed with ADHD.

Specialists use a variety of tests to see if a child has a learning disability.

The specialists first observed the boys in various situations, especially those requiring attention, focus, and self-control. The specialists also talked with the parents and teachers about the children's behaviors in different settings. ADHD seems to run in families, so they asked about other family members who might show the disorder. In addition, learning disabilities can be mistaken for ADHD and often occur along with ADHD. Therefore, the specialists tested for those as well.

Hyperactive/Impulsive ADHD

Doctors divide ADHD into three types, each with different symptoms. People with the hyperactive/impulsive type are usually super-active. They fidget and squirm, and have trouble sitting still in class or during quiet activities. They act impulsively, often interrupting others and talking when it's not their turn. They may be impatient and seem to be constantly on the go. Because their behaviors can be disruptive, these people are most likely to be referred for ADHD testing.

People with hyperactive/impulsive ADHD are often disruptive in class.

Those with inattentive ADHD may find their minds wandering almost constantly.

Inattentive ADHD

People with inattentive ADHD seem to be the exact opposite. Symptoms include being forgetful and distracted. These people have a hard time focusing their attention and often become bored with projects. They may "zone out" and seem to be daydreaming or not listening when spoken to. They often have trouble following instructions. They also frequently lose or misplace things that they need to complete schoolwork or activities.

Some adults suffer from ADHD just as children do.

Combined ADHD

The third type of ADHD is a combination of the first two. People suffering from combined ADHD experience a range of symptoms. They show hyperactive and impulsive behaviors, as well as inattentive or distracted behaviors. Most people diagnosed with ADHD have this combined form of the disorder.

A Family Affair

Physical features such as hair color and whether a person is left-handed are **inherited**. That is, children get these features from their parents. ADHD also runs in families. Parents with ADHD have a greater than 50 percent chance of having a child with ADHD. About one-quarter of kids with ADHD have parents who also suffer from the disorder. For identical twins, when one twin is diagnosed with ADHD, the other twin has an 80 percent chance of having it as well.

Bad grades are one possible problem caused by ADHD.

CHAPTER 3

What Is ADHD?

We've learned that ADHD causes a variety of symptoms. The disorder can make it difficult to do well in school. It can also affect other situations where self-control and attention are important. But what exactly is ADHD? It was not until the 1980s that doctors included ADHD in the manual they use to diagnose mental disorders. However, doctors as far back as the 1700s have described ADHD-like symptoms in children.

ADHD is a problem that has been around for hundreds of years.

A Problem in the Brain

ADHD is a brain disorder that begins in childhood. It can continue through the teen years and adulthood. Imaging studies have shown that the brains of people with ADHD mature more slowly than those of people without the disorder. This is most noticeable in the brain areas involved in thinking, paying attention, and planning. Other studies have found that certain areas of the brain are slightly smaller and have less activity in people with ADHD.

Brain scans of people without ADHD (below left) and with ADHD (below right) show significant differences in brain activity.

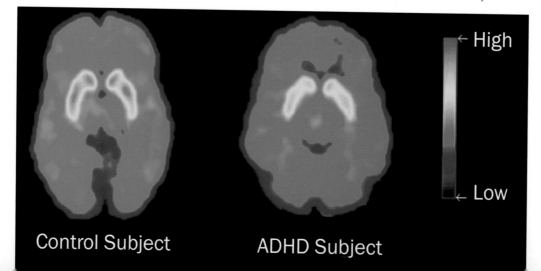

High

Low

Control Subject

ADHD Subject

A parent with ADHD might pass his condition down to his children.

Heredity and Environment

Scientists don't yet know exactly what causes ADHD. It seems that heredity and a person's **environment** both play a role. Researchers have done many studies on families, twins, and families whose members are not biologically related because of adoption. Most studies show that children who have a family member with ADHD are much more likely to have the disorder. Scientists estimate that heredity accounts for 70 to 80 percent of the risk of developing ADHD.

Environmental Risk Factors

Many things in the environment can increase a person's risk of developing ADHD. Some of these factors can occur before birth. Researchers are studying the effects of exposure to cigarette smoke or alcohol during pregnancy. Lead, pesticides, and other environmental **toxins** may also increase the risk of ADHD.

Pesticides and other chemicals can cause a variety of medical conditions, possibly including ADHD.

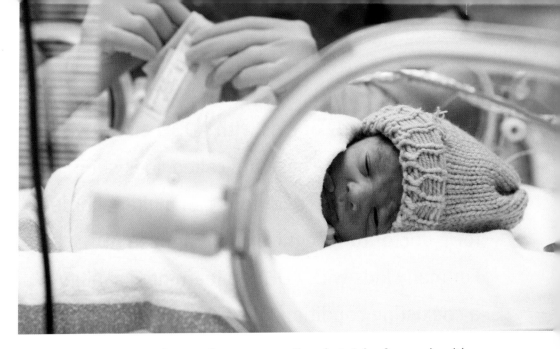

Babies born prematurely are often very small and at risk of many health problems.

Children who were born prematurely or were underweight have a higher risk of ADHD. The same is true for children who have suffered head injuries. People speculate that watching too much TV, eating too much sugar, and playing too many video games cause ADHD. Some people have even suggested that poor parenting is the cause. Some of these factors may worsen a person's symptoms, but there is no evidence they cause ADHD in the first place.

Related Problems

About two-thirds of kids with ADHD also have other difficulties. These are called coexisting conditions. These conditions can make it harder for a doctor to recognize and diagnose ADHD. For many kids with ADHD, a learning disability is a coexisting condition. The most common ones affect reading and writing, and can contribute to a child's struggles at school.

Timeline of ADHD Discovery

1902

Sir George Still conducts the first scientific studies of symptoms now considered to be ADHD.

1937

The U.S. government approves the first drug for use in treating ADHD symptoms.

Other conditions that often go along with ADHD are anxiety and mood disorders. A child with anxiety may be fearful or panicky. Physical symptoms include a racing heart or stomach pains. A mood disorder may result in quickly changing moods, feelings of isolation, and aggressive behavior. Forty percent of kids with ADHD also have oppositional defiant disorder. They behave stubbornly, have angry outbursts, and often break school or family rules.

1968
ADHD symptoms are added to the official manual used in diagnosing diseases as "hyperkinetic reaction of childhood."

1980
Doctors begin referring to hyperkinetic reaction as attention deficit disorder (ADD).

1987
ADD officially becomes known as ADHD.

Famous Folks With ADHD

At times, it can be difficult to live with ADHD. The symptoms may make it hard to pay attention in class. It can be even harder to concentrate on homework and other activities. People with ADHD might feel they're not as smart or as talented as other kids. But that's not true! Many people with ADHD are highly successful—some have even become famous! Here are just a few people who were diagnosed with ADHD or showed many symptoms of the disorder.

Albert Einstein — Nobel Prize–winning physicist who developed the general theory of relativity

Leonardo da Vinci — one of the greatest painters of all time. He was also an expert in architecture, science, music, mathematics, engineering, astronomy, and many other fields.

Wolfgang Amadeus Mozart — a famous musician who wrote his first piece of music at the age of five. He composed more than 600 pieces in his lifetime.

Henry Ford — founder of the Ford Motor Company. He was responsible for manufacturing the first car that many middle-class Americans could afford.

Walt Disney — a talented cartoonist, animator, and film producer. He was the founder of the Walt Disney entertainment empire.

Earvin "Magic" Johnson — a legendary basketball player who won many awards, including an Olympic gold medal

John F. Kennedy — the 35th president of the United States

Talking to a psychologist or some other specialist can help people with ADHD control their symptoms.

CHAPTER 4

Treating ADHD

The specialists diagnosed both Brian and Carl with ADHD. Brian was found to have inattentive ADHD. This explained his forgetfulness and inability to concentrate. Carl was diagnosed with combined ADHD. He showed some symptoms of inattention. Most of his behaviors, however, were typical of the hyperactive/impulsive form of the disorder.

Medication and therapy can help a person cope with ADHD.

Medication can help fight many of the problems caused by ADHD.

Treatment Options

There is no cure for ADHD. There are, however, many ways of treating and managing the disorder. These treatments can help make life easier for the person with ADHD, as well as for his or her family. For very young children, the recommended treatment is usually therapy. Specialized therapy helps change the behaviors that are causing problems. For older children, doctors often recommend a combination of behavior therapy and medication.

Behavior Therapy

Behavior therapy helps people with ADHD learn to manage the way they act. It encourages positive behaviors and discourages disruptive or other problem behaviors. For example, a teacher may reward a child for raising his hand in class. When the student interrupts or yells, the teacher may impose consequences, such as a time out. Over time, the child's behavior can improve.

Behavior therapy takes time and effort to work.

Behavior therapy is most effective when it is used in all areas of a child's daily life. This includes at school, at home, and in other social situations. Parents, teachers, and doctors or counselors must work together to set behavior goals for a child with ADHD. A person's behavior will not change overnight. It may feel as if ADHD symptoms will never go away. The trick is to keep at it and stay positive.

Honest communication with family members, friends, and teachers can help people manage their ADHD symptoms.

Medication such as Adderall might be prescribed to help people with ADHD concentrate better.

Medications for ADHD

For some kids, a combination of therapy and medication is the best way to manage ADHD. The most commonly prescribed medications are ones that **stimulate** a person's brain. It may seem odd to treat someone who is hyperactive and impulsive with a stimulating drug. However, researchers have found people with ADHD don't have enough of certain chemicals in their brains.

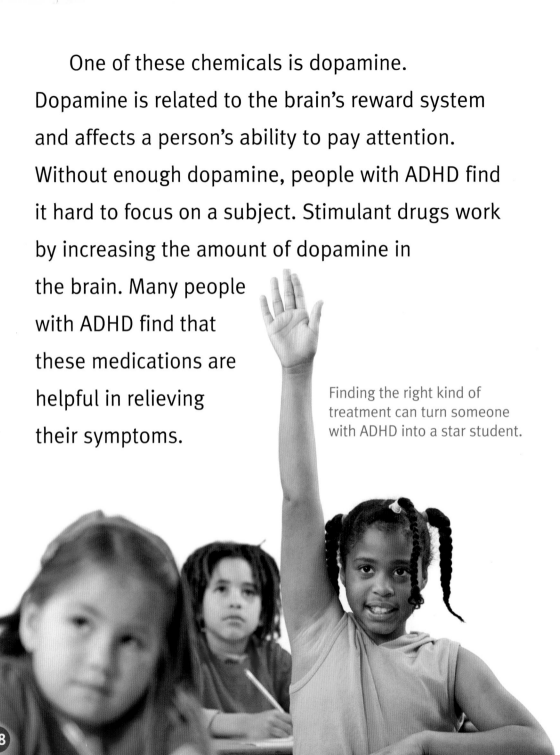

One of these chemicals is dopamine. Dopamine is related to the brain's reward system and affects a person's ability to pay attention. Without enough dopamine, people with ADHD find it hard to focus on a subject. Stimulant drugs work by increasing the amount of dopamine in the brain. Many people with ADHD find that these medications are helpful in relieving their symptoms.

Finding the right kind of treatment can turn someone with ADHD into a star student.

Side Effects

ADHD medications can be helpful, but they often come with unpleasant side effects. Some common ones are nervousness, anxiety, and difficulty sleeping. A patient may also suffer a loss of appetite, nausea, and dizziness. Figuring out how to manage ADHD is a big decision. Every parent with a child who suffers from ADHD must carefully weigh the good and bad aspects of each treatment.

Even hanging out and having fun with friends can be hard sometimes for people who suffer from ADHD.

CHAPTER 5

Living With ADHD

What is it like to live with ADHD? Many kids describe feeling restless and jumpy, as though their bodies and brains are on overdrive. Some kids are very talkative and act out in class. Even though they know these behaviors will get them into trouble and irritate their friends, they can't stop. ADHD sufferers may find it almost impossible to concentrate on something that doesn't interest them.

 ADHD affects not just school, but all areas of a person's life.

ADHD and Loved Ones

Do you have a friend or family member who has ADHD? Knowing that certain behaviors are symptoms of the disorder can help you be more understanding. Perhaps your friend interrupts you several times during a conversation. Maybe he or she doesn't seem to listen to what you have to say. By learning about ADHD, you may find it easier to accept and understand the behavior.

If you have a friend or sibling with ADHD, be patient and try helping him or her concentrate on homework and other important tasks.

Living with ADHD presents challenges, but they can be overcome.

If you have ADHD, it can be reassuring to know that you are not "bad" or "stupid" or "lazy." The feelings and behaviors you struggle with are not your fault. You will always have ADHD. But your symptoms, especially hyperactivity, may lessen over time. It takes patience, therapy, support from your family and friends, and maybe medication. You can go on to live a successful and happy life. ★

Number of children in the United States who have been diagnosed with ADHD: 6.4 million

Average age when a child is diagnosed with ADHD: 7 years old

Percent of children with ADHD who also suffer from another condition, such as a learning disability, anxiety, or depression: 66

Percent of people whose childhood ADHD symptoms continue into adulthood: Up to 60

Likelihood that a child with an identical twin with ADHD will also be diagnosed with ADHD: 80 percent

Did you find the truth?

F There is only one type of ADHD.

T Experts do not fully understand what causes ADHD.

Resources

Books

Spodak, Ruth, and Kenneth Stefano. *Take Control of ADHD: The Ultimate Guide for Teens With ADHD*. Waco, TX: Prufrock Press, 2011.

Taylor, John F. *The Survival Guide for Kids With ADHD*. Golden Valley, MN: Free Spirit Publishing, 2013.

Visit this Scholastic Web site for more information on ADHD:

 www.factsfornow.scholastic.com

Enter the keyword **ADHD**

Important Words

diagnose (dye-uhg-NOHS) determine what disease a patient has or what the cause of a problem is

disorder (dis-OR-dur) a physical or mental illness

environment (en-VYE-ruhn-muhnt) all the things that are part of your life and have an effect on it, such as your family, your school, the place where you live, and the events that happen to you

hyperactivity (hye-pur-ak-TIV-uh-tee) the state of being extremely active or too active

inattentive (in-uh-TEN-tiv) not paying attention

inherited (in-HER-ut-ed) received a particular characteristic from a parent

learning disabilities (LUR-ning dis-uh-BIL-uh-teez) conditions that affect the brain and interfere with a person's ability to learn

stimulate (STIM-yuh-late) encourage something to become more active

toxins (TAHK-sinz) poisonous or harmful substances

Index

Page numbers in **bold** indicate illustrations.

About the Author

Ann O. Squire is a psychologist and an animal behaviorist. Before becoming a writer, she studied the behavior of rats, tropical fish in the Caribbean, and electric fish from central Africa. Her favorite part of being a writer is the chance to learn as much as she can about all sorts of topics. In addition to *ADHD* and books on other health topics, Dr. Squire has written about many different animals, from lemmings to leopards and cicadas to cheetahs. She lives in Asheville, North Carolina.